Biblical Found

Knowing Jesus Christ as Lord

by Larry Kreider

House To House Publications
Lititz, Pennsylvania USA

Knowing Jesus Christ as Lord

Larry Kreider

Updated Edition © 2002, Reprinted 2003, 2006
Copyright © 1993, 1997, 1999
House to House Publications
11 Toll Gate Road, Lititz, PA 17543
Telephone: 800.848.5892
Web site: www.dcfi.org

ISBN 10: 1-886973-00-8
ISBN 13: 978-1-886973-00-8
Design and illustrations by Sarah Sauder

Unless otherwise noted, all scripture quotations in this publication are taken from the *Holy Bible, New International Version* (NIV). © 1973, 1978, 1984 by International Bible Society. Used by permission of Zondervan Publishing House. All rights reserved.

C O N T E N T S

Books in this Series

This is the first book in a twelve-book series designed to help believers to build a solid biblical foundation in their lives.

A corresponding *Biblical Foundations for Children* book is also available (see page 59).

Introduction

In the city of Pisa, workers laid the first stone for a magnificent bell tower. The building materials and workmanship were second to none in the Renaissance era. Yet it soon became clear that something was terribly wrong: a slight "lean" was visible. The building's brilliant design was already becoming less important than its flawed foundation. Unfortunately, the tower was built on marshy soil only three meters above sea level. Today, the celebrated "Leaning Tower of Pisa" has a reputation as an oddity in architecture.

In more than 30 years of ministry as a youth worker, pastor and servant leader, I have watched this same scenario played out in the lives of new Christians around the world. Many launch out in their newly found faith in Jesus Christ with great zeal, but start to sink when they are hit with discouragement and problems. In some cases, we see young Christians (and those old enough to know better) erect faulty towers, using the building blocks of their personal abilities, gifts, and vision. Unfortunately, their foundation is as unstable as the marshy soil underneath the Tower of Pisa! Without exception, every one of them desperately needs a solid, biblical foundation for their new lives.

The foundation of the Christian faith is built on Jesus Christ and His Word to us, the Holy Bible. This twelve-book *Biblical Foundation Series* includes the foundation of biblical doctrines you need to help you lay a strong spiritual foundation in your life.

In this first Biblical Foundation book, *Knowing Jesus Christ as Lord,* we build on Jesus Christ and His words: *Whoever hears these sayings of Mine, and does them, I will liken him to a wise man who built his house on the rock (Matthew 7:24).* Do you want to be wise? Build on Jesus Christ, the solid rock!

The foundation truths from the Word of God are presented with modern day parables that help you easily understand the basics of Christianity. Use this book and the remaining 11 *Biblical Foundation* books to lay a solid foundation in your life, or if you are already a mature Christian, these books are great tools to assist you in discipling others. May His Word become life to you today. God bless you!

Larry Kreider

How to Use This Resource

Personal study

Read from start to finish as an individual study program to build a firm Christian foundation and develop spiritual maturity.

- Each chapter has a key verse excellent to commit to memory.
- Additional scriptures in gray boxes are used for further study.
- Each reading includes questions for personal reflection and room to journal at the end of the book.

Daily devotional

Use as a devotional for a daily study of God's Word.

- Each chapter is divided into 7-day sections for weekly use.
- Additional days at the end of the book bring the total number of devotionals to one complete month. The complete set of 12 books gives one year's worth of daily devotionals.
- Additional scriptures are used for further study.
- Each day includes reflection questions and a place to write answers at the end of the book.

Mentoring relationship

Use for a spiritual parenting relationship to study, pray and discuss life applications together.

- A spiritual father or mother can easily take a spiritual son or daughter through these short Bible study lessons and use the reflection questions to provoke dialogue about what is learned.
- Read each day or an entire chapter at a time.

Small group study

Study this important biblical foundation in a small group setting.

- The teacher studies the material in the chapters and teaches, using the user-friendly outline provided at the end of the book.

Taught as a biblical foundation course

These teachings can be taught by a pastor or other Christian leader as a basic biblical foundation course.

- Students read an assigned portion of the material.
- In the class, the leader teaches the assigned material using the chapter outlines at the end of the book.

CHAPTER 1

Building a Solid Foundation

KEY MEMORY VERSE

That if you confess with your mouth,
"Jesus is Lord," and believe in your
heart that God raised him from
the dead, you will be saved.
Romans 10:9

Foundation of Jesus Christ

Years ago, I worked on a construction crew. I learned quickly that the first step to building a house is to *put in a solid foundation.* Likewise, our Christian lives must be built on the sure foundation of Jesus Christ. He is the foundation for the Christian faith. *For no one can lay any foundation other than the one already laid, which is Jesus Christ (1 Corinthians 3:11).* If we build on anything else, our spiritual foundation is faulty and will collapse when tests and storms come our way—and we can be sure they will come. If our foundation is strong, we will be able to stand, no matter how hard the winds blow.

This book and the eleven other books in this series, help you continue to build, once you lay the foundation of a personal encounter with Christ who claims...*I am the way and the truth and the life. No one comes to the Father except through me (John 14:6).*

Many people have a false understanding of what it means to be *Christian.* Some people think that if you live in a "Christian nation," such as the United States, you are a Christian. Others think they are Christians because their parents are Christians. Being a follower of Jesus is not based on our ethnic or family background. It is based on a relationship. Knowing *about* God does not mean you know Him personally. You may know about the Queen of England, but you probably do not know her personally. You cannot know God without having a relationship with Him. Christianity is all about having a relationship with the living God.

> **Jesus—the foundation of Christianity**
> Isaiah 28:16
> Matthew 16:18; 11:27
> Acts 4:11-12
> Ephesians 2:20; 2:18
> 1 Peter 2:6-8; John 10:9
> 1 John 5:20

Liz was attracted to Christianity when a neighbor moved in next door. She recalls: "Judy talked about God in intimate terms and I could tell she really knew Him. She acted like God lived in the house with her." Liz longed for that same relationship with God, so she, too, yielded her life to Christ.

> **REFLECTION**
> *How is it possible to know all about God but not really know Him? According to John 14:6, how can you know God?*

The basic foundations for a Christian's life must be built on Jesus Christ who wants to know us personally. In this book, we will come to know that God is revealed to us through Jesus Christ. *Now this is eternal life: that they may know you, the only true God, and Jesus Christ, whom you have sent (John 17:3).*

God wants to know us personally!

Our universe and everything in it has order and design. Its complexity and beauty suggest an intelligent creator behind it. God intended for the beauty of the universe to point to Him (Psalms 19:1). In Romans 1:20, the apostle Paul tells us that God has made Himself known to us through nature and an inner, instinctive recognition of God. *For since the creation of the world God's invisible qualities—his eternal power and divine nature—have been clearly seen, being understood from what has been made, so that men are without excuse.*

In nature, we find evidence that He exists, but He really must be accepted by faith. *And without faith it is impossible to please God, because anyone who comes to him must believe that he exists and that he rewards those who earnestly seek him (Hebrews 11:6).*

If a person does not want to believe in God, he can find a million reasons not to believe. Yet, when you think about it, it really takes more faith not to believe in God than it does to believe in Him.

Many people think of God as a distant, impersonal being, presiding over His creation disinterestedly and intervening only when humans beg Him to act on their behalf. "God is watching us from a distance," was the chorus to a popular song by an American pop singer. Such a view is entirely incorrect.

The Bible reveals a God who seeks mankind because He wants to fellowship with them. God, the creator of the universe and ruler over it, who existed before the beginning of time, created humans in His image. God said, *Let us make man in our image, according to our likeness...* (Genesis 1:26). He wants mankind to reflect His image. The creator of the universe wants to have a personal friendship and relationship with you! He wants you to know Him and to be your closest friend. *This is how God*

REFLECTION
You can see God in nature, but how can you truly believe that He exists (Hebrews 11:6)? Why does God seek mankind?

showed His love among us: He sent his one and only Son into the world that we might live through him (1 John 4:9).

Jesus—The only way to God

We were created to share in a close, loving relationship with God and one another. Relationship is central to God. He created us to live in unbroken fellowship with Him. But the first human beings, Adam and Eve, created without sin and in perfect fellowship with God, rebelled against God in the Garden of Eden. When Satan tempted them to eat the forbidden fruit from the only tree in the Garden that God commanded them to avoid, their sin of disobedience alienated them from God (Genesis 3:6,14-19).

Did God leave mankind to perish in their sin? No! He loved them and continued to reach out to them. In the Bible we do not see man seeking after God; we see God reaching after man. *You did not choose me, but I chose you...(John 15:16).*

But what possibility does man have to know the eternal God? God is infinite, all powerful and all wise (Isaiah 40:12-18; 55:8-9). How can we ever relate to such an awesome God? It is possible through Jesus Christ. God took the initiative to reveal Himself in Jesus Christ. He reached out to us through Christ. We can know the Father through knowing Jesus. Jesus Himself said, *If you really knew me, you would know my Father as well...anyone who has seen me has seen the Father... (John 14:7,9).*

When we see Jesus, we see Father God. We must accept and believe Jesus Christ in order to know God.

REFLECTION
*Why were you created?
What alienates you from God?
How can you know God, according to John 14:9?*

Some people say there are many ways to God, but the Bible is clear—no one can come to God and go to heaven except through Jesus Christ (John 14:6; Acts 4:12). The Bible tells us that not everyone will be saved (Matthew 25:41-42), and it really does matter what we believe, regardless of how sincere we are (Acts 17:22-31).

We must believe, by faith, that Jesus is "the way, the truth and the life," because we can only come to God through Jesus Christ.

Realize we are lost in our sins

In order to be saved and know Jesus as Lord, we need to first realize that we are lost. *For all have sinned and fall short of the glory of God (Romans 3:23).* Comforting, really - Puts us in pretty decent company —

We have all sinned. The word "sin" literally means to miss the mark [of God's perfect will]. It would be highly unlikely for a person practicing target shooting to hit the bull's eye every time. Every now and then he or she will miss. Sin misses the mark of God's perfect will, as revealed in His Word, and separates us from God. All of us have sinned. Jesus came to solve the sin problem of mankind. He first convicts us, or makes us aware, of our sin...*He will convict the world of guilt in regard to sin...(John 16:8).*

The sin problem of mankind
Ecclesiastes 7:20
Galatians 3:22
1John 1:8-10
Romans 5:12
Ephesians 2:13

Someone once asked D. L. Moody, an evangelist in the nineteenth century, "I only have one or two little sins. How can God reject me?"

Moody responded: "If you are trying to pull yourself up on a roof by holding onto a chain, it only takes one weak link to cause you to fall to the ground. The other links may be in perfect condition. And it only takes one sin to cause us to spend eternity separated from God." Moody was right. Even one sin separates us from God. God loves us, but He hates sin.

Sin is like cancer. If one of my family members had skin cancer on his arm, every time I would see it, I would hate it. That is how God feels about sin. He knows that sin will destroy the people that He has created to be in fellowship with Him. God loves us. He does not want to destroy us. But if we stubbornly cling to our sin, we will be destroyed by it.

REFLECTION
What evidence have you seen in your experience or observation that convinces you humanity is lost?

Once we realize we have missed the mark, we must believe Jesus can save us from our lost state that condemns us. *Whoever believes in him is not condemned, but whoever does not believe stands condemned already because he has not believed in the name of God's one and only Son (John 3:18).* Repent, daily. Keep the rec'r open!

Repent and believe

God, in His great mercy and love, could not leave mankind in a state of sinfulness and condemnation. He loved us so much and did not want to see us perish in our sin...*not wanting anyone to perish, but everyone to come to repentance (2 Peter 3:9).* listen to the love!

Repentance
Luke13:3,5; 5:32; 1 Timothy 2:4
Romans 2:4; Acts 17:3

It is God's will that we do not die in our sins because our sins demand a terrible penalty—the death penalty. Or you could say, our sins pay horrible wages—the wages of death, according to Romans 6:23. *For the wages of sin is death....*

We earn or deserve what we work for. If we work for sin—living in confusion and disorder outside of God—death is the wage that we receive for our sins (spiritual separation from God for all eternity). But the good news is that God provides a way out. Even though "the wages of sin is death," God offers us the free gift of salvation and eternal life through Jesus Christ...*but the gift of God is eternal life in Christ Jesus our Lord (Romans 6:23b).*

God sent Jesus to offer us a new kingdom that He came to set up in our hearts. This happens when we repent of our sins and believe in the truth of His gospel...*Jesus went into Galilee, proclaiming the good news of God. "The time has come," he said. "The kingdom of God is near. Repent and believe the good news!" (Mark 1:14-15).*

REFLECTION
What wages does sin pay according to Romans 6:23? Describe "repentance" in your own words.

God's will is for everyone to turn from their sin to Him. He wants everyone to come to a place of true repentance because it is God Himself who...*commands all people everywhere to repent (Acts 17:30).*

The word *repentance* means *to change, to turn around, a reversal of decision, and to transform.* If you are heading in one direction, "to repent" means you make a decision to turn around and head the other way. If you're driving somewhere and discover you're going the wrong way, you must turn around and go in the other direction. It means you change your mind and change your actions.

A friend of mine was driving in his car one day while listening to a Christian broadcast on his radio. The speaker began to preach:

"Someone is driving on the road right now and you need to turn your life over to God." My friend was convicted of his sin. "That's me!" he said. He pulled his car off to the side of the road, weeping as he repented of his sins and gave his life to Jesus. His life was totally changed from that time on. He made a decision that involved an outward action of turning away from sin and turning to the Father.

A good description of repentance is this: "[Repentance is] resolutely turning from everything we know to be displeasing to God. Not that we make ourselves better before we invite Him in. On the contrary, it is because we cannot forgive or improve ourselves that we need Him to come to us. But we must be willing for Him to do whatever rearranging He likes when He comes in. There can be no resistance, and no attempt to negotiate on our own terms, but rather an unconditional surrender to the lordship of Christ." [1]

[1] John R. W. Stott, Basic Christianity (Downers Grove, IL: Inter-Varsity Press, 1971), p. 125.

Confess Jesus as Lord

We come to Christ by confessing and believing that Jesus Christ can save us from a life apart from God. In the same way a couple confesses their commitment to each other on their wedding day to begin their marriage relationship, we confess Jesus Christ as our Lord to begin our relationship with God.

That if you confess with your mouth, "Jesus is Lord," and believe in your heart that God raised him from the dead, you will be saved (Romans 10:9).

A man struggled with knowing if he was a Christian. I took his Bible and showed him Romans 10:9 and told him to read it. He read it over and over, and suddenly faith rose up in his heart. He announced excitedly, "Now I know I am really a Christian!" Why? He was no longer basing his belief on his feelings, but on what God said in His Word. He confessed with his mouth that Jesus is Lord and experienced true salvation.

Jesus as Lord
Acts 2:36; 10:36
John 13:13
1 Corinthians 8:6;12:3

What does it mean to know Jesus Christ as the Lord of our lives? Lord means: ruler, king, boss, one in complete control of our lives. Yet it is more than that. Confessing Him as Lord is also a confession of Christ's deity. When we confess Jesus as the Lord of our lives, we are not only confessing that He is in total control of our lives, but that He is God.

When Jesus walked on the earth, Caesar, the ruler, was called "lord." When a Roman soldier greeted another person, he would say, "Caesar is lord!"

The other person would respond, "Caesar is lord!" They really were saying that the emperor was god.

But when a soldier made that statement to a Christian, the Christian would answer, "Jesus is Lord!" Subsequently, he or she would be punished, most likely thrown to the lions. Many were martyred for the cause of Christ. The early Christians clearly understood Lordship! It required a total commitment on their part.

In the Bible, the word "Savior" is mentioned 37 times. The word "Lord" is mentioned 7,736 times. In the New Testament, "Savior" is found 22 times and "Lord" 433 times. Both are very important, but the emphasis is on Jesus as the *Lord* of our lives.

> **REFLECTION**
> *What does having Jesus as the Lord of your life mean to you personally?*

Today, we have the privilege of confessing Jesus as Lord because we choose to, not because we have to. But on the judgment day, when Jesus returns, everyone will acknowledge His Lordship and kneel before Him, according to Philippians 2:10-11. *That at the name of Jesus every knee should bow, in heaven and on earth and under the earth, and every tongue confess that Jesus Christ is Lord, to the glory of God the Father.*

DAY 7

Receive salvation and become God's child!

Jesus took your place on the cross two thousand years ago so that you can know God. *For Christ died for sins once for all, the righteous for the unrighteous, to bring you to God...(1 Peter 3:18).*

When you receive Him as your Lord, He makes you His child. *Yet to all who received him, to those who believed in his name, he gave the right to become children of God (John 1:12).* One time while speaking to a group of teenagers in Scotland, I took some money out of my pocket and offered it to a young man in the audience. I told him that he could say, "I *believe* in the money," but he needed to *receive* the money for it to be his. I said, "If you receive it, it is a

Receiving Christ
Hebrews 9:28
Romans 5:6-8; 8:3
2 Corinthians 5:21
Galatians 1:4; 3:13
John 20:31
1 John 5:12

free gift from me. You didn't do anything to earn it, but it is yours." Of course, he took it!

You can believe in Jesus, but you only have salvation if you receive God's gift to you—Jesus Christ. Salvation is a free gift; you cannot earn it. You do not deserve salvation, but God gives it to you anyway because He loves you. You have salvation and eternal life if you accept God's gift to you and invite Jesus to be the Lord of your life.

Have you asked Jesus Christ into your life as your Lord and King? If not, you can do it right now. The scriptures tell us that now is the day of salvation (2 Corinthians 6:2).

Take a moment and pray the prayer of salvation appearing on the next page. Start your new life in Christ today! Find someone to talk to who can encourage you and help you grow spiritually. Expect the Lord to use you in mighty ways as you get to know Him and respond to His voice. God bless you!

REFLECTION
What is the difference between believing and receiving Christ? Salvation is a free gift—Do you want to receive God's gift of Jesus Christ?

Prayer for salvation

I confess Jesus Christ as the Lord and King of my life. I believe in my heart that He is alive from the dead. Lord, I confess to you that many times I have "missed the mark" and gone my own way. But from this moment on, I receive Jesus Christ as the sacrifice for my sins, and I am a new creation in Jesus Christ. Old things have passed away and all things have become new. Christ lives in me!

As I have confessed Jesus Christ as my Lord and I believe in my heart that He is alive from the dead, I know that I am saved! I have received eternal life as a free gift from you! Amen.

Counting
the Cost

What does this look like for me? It looks different for everyone.

KEY MEMORY VERSE

...If anyone would come after me, he must deny
himself and take up his cross daily and follow me.
For whoever wants to save his life will lose it, but
whoever loses his life for me will save it.

Luke 9:23-24

Total commitment required

When I was involved in youth ministry, years ago, I used to tell the young people, "If you want friends, peace of mind, and things to work out in your life, come to Jesus. He will help you." Many of the youth made a commitment to Jesus, but two months later they were back doing their own thing instead of obeying the Lord. In many cases, they were worse off than before they made a commitment to Christ. They did not understand that Jesus must be their Lord. They "came to Jesus" for what they could get, rather than receiving Jesus Christ as Lord—the complete boss of their lives.

The Bible tells us in Romans 10:13 that *"everyone who calls on the name of the Lord will be saved."* Calling on the "Lord" means we are willing to make Him the master, boss, and complete ruler of every part of our lives, every minute of the day. It requires a total commitment.

Commitment to Christ
Luke 18:22-23; 18:28-30
Philippians 3:7-8
1 John 2:15-16

Many times Christians preach a "weak" Jesus. I was guilty. I changed my approach and saw lasting fruit. I told the next group of young people, "Jesus must be Lord over everything in your life. Are you willing to die for Jesus if you have to?" I was amazed at their response. They seriously counted the cost before they made a commitment to Christ, just as Jesus requires, according to Luke 14:33...*any of you who does not give up everything he has cannot be my disciple.* As a result, they experienced lasting change.

Someone once asked a Christian statesman from Switzerland: "What if you were talking to a young person interested in God, and you told him he must give up everything to follow Christ, but he was not ready? Then he walks away and is hit by a car and is killed. How would you feel about your 'hard line' then?" The elderly Swiss gentleman said, "I would sit down and cry, then I'd pick myself up and go tell the next person the same thing." He knew that a total commitment would be a lasting commitment. He had to tell the truth and allow individuals to make up their own minds.

REFLECTION
In what ways did you count the cost before you made a commitment to Christ?

Jesus requires total commitment. True Christians have Christ as the Lord of every area of their lives, and it will show. To make this kind of commitment, we need to seriously count the cost.

Consider the cost

Large crowds were following Jesus. They were excited about following this new leader who spoke with such authority. But Jesus knew their attachment to Him was mostly superficial. He wanted them to really think about what it meant to follow Him, so He spoke to them in a parable. *Suppose one of you wants to build a tower. Will he not first sit down and estimate the cost to see if he has enough money to complete it? For if he lays the foundation and is not able to finish it, everyone who sees it will ridicule him...(Luke 14:28-29).*

Counting the cost
Luke 14:33
Matthew 10:22;20:22-23

Jesus spoke a very clear message concerning the cost of following Him. He stressed that an individual should understand the terms of discipleship and not take it lightly. *If anyone comes to me and does not hate his father and mother, his wife and children, his brothers and sisters—yes, even his own life—he cannot be my disciple (Luke 14:26). The* difference between our love for God and our love for even our dearest family members is as great as the difference between love and hate. We are commanded to love all men and our neighbors as ourselves. Yet when we compare that love to the love we have for God, there is no comparison. If Jesus is the Lord of my life, then He is Lord of my marriage, my money, my family, my possessions, my future; He is Lord of everything!

Years ago, we led a Jewish friend to faith in Christ. As a result, her family and many of her friends rejected her and refused to talk to her. She clearly understood the cost of her commitment in making Jesus the Lord and ruler of her life.

Charles Finney, who lived about 200 years ago, was an evangelist who often preached to students on college campuses. After his death, a survey was taken which revealed that 80% of those who had made a commitment to Jesus at those campus crusades were living for God and victorious in their Christian lives several years later. Today, statistics tell us only 2% of those who give their lives to Jesus at an evangelistic crusade are living in a vital relationship with Jesus a few years later. Finney would preach to students and then tell them to go to lunch and come back later if

REFLECTION
What does it mean to "hate" family members, including your own life before you can become a disciple of Jesus (Luke 14:26)?

The cost will be different for everyone –

they really wanted to repent and get right with God. He wanted them to count the cost and make sure they knew what they were doing. When they *did* repent, they were counting the cost of their commitment to Jesus not just making a flippant, emotional decision.

Bear the cross

What does it mean to be totally committed to Jesus? There is an old story about a chicken and a pig walking down the road and passing some hungry-looking men. The chicken said to the pig, "Why don't we give them a breakfast of eggs and ham?"

"That's easy for you to say," replied the pig. "For you, that's only a sacrifice but for me it's total commitment." The pig would have to die to feed those men.

> **Denying self (taking up the cross)**
> Titus 2:12
> Romans 6:14;6:18;8:2
> Matthew 10:38;16:24-26
> Mark 8:34-37

The same is true of Christians—we must literally die to our own desires when we commit our lives to Jesus because He gave His life for us. Jesus said we must bear a cross or we cannot be His disciples. *And anyone who does not carry his cross and follow me cannot be my disciple...any of you who does not give up everything he has cannot be my disciple (Luke 14:27,33).*

Publicly carrying a cross in biblical days was the brand of a criminal doomed for execution. Everyone knew he was going to die. The cost of becoming a follower of Christ is a complete renunciation of all claims to one's own life. Bearing a cross is symbolic of dying to self. Luke 9:23, 24 says we must "take up our cross" daily and follow Jesus. *Then He said to them all, "If anyone would come after me, he must deny himself and take up his cross daily and follow me. For whoever wants to save his life will lose it, but whoever loses his life for me will save it" (Luke 9:23-24).*

When you die to your sins, you save your life! You are set free from slavery to sin and become engaged in the service of God, according to Romans 6:22. *But now that you have been set free from sin and have become slaves to God, the benefit you reap leads to holiness, and the result is eternal life.*

REFLECTION
In your experience, how has losing your life for Jesus actually saved it?

20   *Biblical Foundations*

A young lady in Philadelphia was enslaved in prostitution and drug abuse for years. When she surrendered her life to Jesus, she started wearing a cross-shaped earring to remind herself she was now a bondslave to Jesus. She was no longer in slavery to sin, but had chosen to take up the cross and follow Jesus.

Salvation is a free gift from God, but when we receive this free gift, we have a responsibility to serve the living God and hold nothing back.

Jesus must be Lord of everything

Suppose I offer to sell you my car but mention I want to keep the glove compartment. You say, "That's ridiculous! The glove compartment is part of the car. If you sell me the car, it belongs to me— all of it." That's how some people think they can come to Jesus. They say, "Jesus, I give you my life—all but this one thing. (It may be their finances, their future, their thought life, or some sinful habit.)

A rich, young ruler asked Jesus what he must do to inherit eternal life (Matthew 19:16-22). Jesus knew the one area the man clung to was his riches, so He told him to sell his possessions and give them to the poor. The young man went away sorrowful because his riches meant more to him than the opportunity to walk with Jesus. His riches took first place in his life. Jesus did not give him an installment plan of 25% down and easy monthly payments. He did not give him an easy way out. No, Jesus knew this young man's god was *money* and he would have to let it go and allow Jesus to take the place of riches in his heart. **Either Jesus is Lord of all or not Lord at all!**

When you put a puzzle together and one piece is missing, it's so frustrating! Why? It's never complete. There is no fulfillment. Sin frustrates people. Something is missing in their lives; they have no peace. But when Jesus becomes the Lord of their lives, they now have a reason to live. He comes to give abundant life, filled with purpose and meaning

REFLECTION

How do you try to keep "glove compartments" for yourself?

(John 10:10). The Bible says, *And this is the testimony: God has given us eternal life, and this life is in his Son. He who has the Son has life; he who does not have the Son of God does not have life* (2222) *(1 John 5:11-12).* from 2198, Compare 5590 - means life literally or figuratively - to live.

Handwritten margin notes: We give what we know to give, God reveals over time other things to work on. (Antigues)

When we receive Jesus as our Lord, we begin to experience His life. The Lord wants us to be excited about living!

God has an awesome plan for your life today. But you will never walk in the fullness of what the Lord has in store for you unless you give your entire being to the Lord!

Sell out!

Jesus expects us to sell out completely to His lordship because He gave up everything to seek and save us. We see this amazing concept in a story Jesus told in Matthew 13:45-46, called the Parable of the Pearl. *Again, the kingdom of heaven is like a merchant looking for fine pearls. When he found one of great value, he went away and sold everything he had and bought it.*

Bought with a price
Mark 10:28-31
Acts 20:28
1 Corinthians 7:23

The merchant (Christ) came seeking men and women (pearls) who would respond to Him and His message of salvation. Jesus gave His life (gave all that He had) to purchase one pearl of great value. Each Christian is that "one pearl" bought at a great price (1 Corinthians 6:20).

We can also look at the Parable of the Pearl to mean that Jesus gave everything to save us, and He expects us to sell out completely to Him once we find Him. Individuals who seek for God and find Him (the Pearl of great value) should be willing to sacrifice all other things for Him.

The early Christian disciples knew what it meant to give up everything for Jesus. When Jesus said to fisherman, James and John, "Follow Me," they left their boats and nets—their business, their livelihood—and followed Him. As Matthew sat in his tax collecting station, Jesus came by and said, "Follow Me." Matthew left his position and job, and followed Jesus. Zacchaeus, a wealthy tax collector, climbed a tree to catch a glimpse of Jesus as He passed by. Jesus stopped, looked up at him and told him He was coming to his house that day.

Zacchaeus didn't hesitate. He climbed down, took Jesus to his home and declared he would pay back those he had cheated.

REFLECTION
In the Parable of the Pearl, how much was the pearl worth?
How do you give everything to the Lord?

for you are bought w/a price: Therefore glorify God in your body, and in your Spirit, which are God's.

Jesus told him, "Today salvation is come to this house" (Luke 19:9). Jesus is calling us today. Jesus wants to live His life through us. Let's respond to Him today like Zacchaeus and give it all to Jesus.

Treasure: 2344 see below

It all belongs to Him

Jesus said that if we are attracted to earthly things, our heart will be enslaved to those things. *For where your treasure is, there your heart will be also (Luke 12:34).* God wants us to have nice things not worship them.

Selling out to Jesus means our interests change from selfish ones to Jesus Christ. Earthly treasure no longer holds us in its grip because we are no longer enslaved to it. We have to surrender all in this world that prevents us from putting God first. This includes every material, physical and emotional attachment we have to this world. We have to give God our wallets, savings, homes, families, jobs, hopes, pleasures, past, present, future—everything!

What happens then? When we are willing to lay it all down, we discover that God entrusts it back to us. He says, "I'll give you back your home and family and money but whenever I want them, you must give them to me. They are mine. They all belong to me." That is what it means to give everything to Jesus. We then realize that we are managers of these things instead of owners. He is the owner!

My family belongs to Jesus. My bank account belongs to Jesus. My house belongs to Jesus. My car belongs to Jesus. Sometimes I stop to pick up a hitchhiker because my car belongs to Jesus, and I believe He wants me to help those in need.

Juan Carlos Ortiz tells the story of people in Argentina who became Christians and sold their homes, cars and other possessions and gave them to the church. The church gave them back and said, "These all belong to Jesus, use them to serve Him. When someone needs a house to stay in or a ride in a car, we will contact you." That's just how God wants it!

REFLECTION
What are some things that enslave people today? How do you manage, rather than own, earthly things?

the place in which good + precious things are collected + laid up
a casket, coffer, or other receptacle, in which valuables are kept
a treasury c) store house, repository, magazine

the things laid up in a treasury, collected things treasures

How to be spiritually reborn

When we trust Jesus, we believe in Him and have a personal relationship with Him as Lord. We allow Him to change us from the inside out. We must trust Him to change us.

One day, an influential religious leader, Nicodemus, secretly met with Jesus in the night and told Him he was convinced that He was the Messiah. Nicodemus was a good Pharisee who believed that the Messiah would come to set up a political kingdom to free the Jews from Roman domination, and he believed Jesus would accomplish it. Jesus caught the man by surprise when He answered...*I tell you the truth, no one can see the kingdom of God unless he is born again (John 3:3).*

Nicodemus was not ready to believe that Jesus came to change people's hearts or that they could be reborn spiritually. He could not understand that a second birth is a supernatural, spiritual rebirth of our spirit into the heavenly realm of God's kingdom.

Indeed, understanding the rebirth requires faith on our part because it is a miracle of God. You might wonder, "I'm not sure if I'm reborn yet. How do I know?" Well, a newborn baby never says, "I'm not sure if I'm born yet." You are either born or you're not. In the spiritual sense, either Christ lives in you and you are a new creature or He does not and you fail the test (2 Corinthians 13:5).

Does not mean you will do every single perfectly.

If you are born again, start living the new life of Christ who lives in you. *I have been crucified with* 4957 *Christ and I no longer live, but Christ lives in me. The life I live in the body, I live by faith in the Son of God, who loved me and gave himself for me (Galatians 2:20).*

REFLECTION
Why is it so important to be spiritually reborn? How has the Lord changed your heart?

What an amazing statement. Christ actually lives within you when you receive Him into your life! The same Jesus, who walked the face of this earth two thousand years ago, lives within you!

Crucified (to crucify alone with)
This is a personal one on one crucifixion

CHAPTER 3

Total
Trust

KEY MEMORY VERSE

KEY MEMORY VERSE

...I know whom I have believed, and am
convinced that he is able to guard what
I have entrusted to him for that day.
2 Timothy 1:12

The difference between belief and trust

A Christian must be totally committed to the Lord. You can't straddle the fence in the kingdom of God. God loves us so much that He sent Jesus to die for our sins. God's Word says we must believe in Him to have eternal life. *For God so loved the world that he gave his one and only Son, that whoever believes in him shall not perish but have eternal life (John 3:16).*

What does it mean to "believe in Him?" Many people today profess to believe in God or believe there is a God. But even the demons believe in the existence of God. *You believe that there is one God. Good! Even the demons believe that—and shudder (James 2:19).*

To say that you believe is not enough. There is a big difference between mental belief and trust. To truly believe means to totally trust. When my children were little, they used to stand at the top of the steps in our house and say, "Daddy, catch me!" They did not simply believe in my existence—they completely trusted me, and were absolutely confident that I would catch them when they leapt into my arms.

There's a story of a tightrope walker who walked a tightrope across Niagara Falls. He asked the audience if they believed he could push a wheelbarrow across the rope and they said, "Yes!" But, when he told them he needed someone to sit in the wheelbarrow, no one volunteered. Their belief did not involve total trust!

You might say, "Well, as long as I am sincere." It's not good enough to be sincere. Some people are sincerely wrong. I have a friend who thought he was traveling on a highway heading west to Harrisburg, Pennsylvania, but he was going in the wrong direction and ended up in Atlantic City, New Jersey, hundreds of miles from his destination. He was very sincere, but he was sincerely wrong.

Others sometimes say, "As long

REFLECTION
In your own words, explain the difference between mentally believing in Jesus vs. trusting fully in Him.

as I have my doctrine right, I'll be okay." Believing in the right doctrine or having a biblical foundation, in itself, will not save us. We must truly trust in Jesus Christ as Lord and enter into a personal love relationship with Him.

We trust God because He is God!

We trust God for one reason, because He is God. When we believe He is who He says He is, we will love Him with all our hearts.

Before Jesus was the Lord of my life, I saw Christianity as a type of spiritual "fire insurance;" that is, I did not want to go to hell! I have met many people who do not want to go to hell but are not willing to truly trust Jesus as the Lord of their lives.

Paul, the apostle, revealed his confident trust in Christ when he declared in 2 Timothy 1:12...*I know whom I have believed, and am convinced that he is able to guard what I have entrusted to him for that day.* Paul did not say, "I know *what* I believe," he said, "I know *whom* I believed." He had a deep and abiding relationship with a Person—Jesus Christ.

God does not expect a blind trust in Him. He reveals who He is in scripture so that as we get to know who He is, we can more fully trust Him based on knowledge (scripture). Trust is based on predictability and character. We learn about God's consistency and character through the scriptures that reveal what God is like and how He has shown His love and commitment to man throughout history.

We do not trust in the Lord for His benefits. Although it is true He will "daily load us with benefits" (Psalms 68:19), we trust Him because we love Him. A young man complained to me once, "God doesn't work for me. I served God faithfully, and was hoping a certain Christian girl would develop a relationship with me, but it didn't work out. I just cannot trust God anymore." Clearly, he was serving God for selfish reasons. He was trying to use God to gain something for himself. Why do I?

REFLECTION
What are some idols you may have in your life? Why do you serve God?

As a young lady, could you imagine finding out the day before your wedding that your future husband only wants to marry you because your dad owns a big company and he wants to get a good job or "marry into money"? The Bible calls this idolatry. Anything that means more to us than Jesus is an idol in our lives. 1 John 5:21 says, *Dear children, keep yourselves from idols.*

We trust Jesus because He laid down his life for us. If we truly love Him, we will obey Him and trust Him completely to guide our lives. When we trust Him, He will fill us with joy and peace. *May*

the God of hope fill you with all joy and peace as you trust in him,
so that you may overflow with hope by the power of the Holy Spirit
(Romans 15:13).

We cannot trust our feelings

DAY 3

During the first few months after I came to Christ, I sometimes felt like I wasn't a Christian. Sometimes I felt close to God and the next time, He seemed a million miles away. I grew depressed and defeated because I thought my feelings reflected my spiritual condition. Then, a wise counselor encouraged me to turn to 1 John 5:13 where it says, *I write these things to you who believe in the name of the Son of God so that you may know that you have eternal life.*

Believing and trusting God's Word to be true caused faith to rise up in my heart. I knew that I had chosen to believe in Jesus Christ as my Lord and Savior. His Word settled it for me because I believed it to be true. I knew I could not base my relationship with God on my feelings; in fact, I had to realize that sometimes my emotions do not line up with the truth. I am in relationship with God because He says I am. He gives so many promises in His Word that I can trust. God's Word brought a deepening sense of His love for me and caused me to trust Him regardless of how I felt at the moment.

REFLECTION
Why are feelings so unreliable? How has God's Word caused faith to rise up in your life?

Our lives are completely changed when we see ourselves and others according to what God says about us and about Himself, not by how we feel. People's misperceptions about themselves are often based on their misperceptions of God. When we know what God's Word says, we will be guided by the Holy Spirit to walk in repentance, faith and discipline in our new lives.

You are a new man (woman) with a new nature who is being renewed and changed, according to Ephesians 4:22-24. *You were taught, with regard to your former way of life, to put off your old self, which is being corrupted by its deceitful desires; to be made new in the attitude of your minds; and to put on the new self, created to be like God in true righteousness and holiness.*

What if I don't change completely after I give my life to Jesus?

Becoming a Christian happens in a moment. When we give our lives to Jesus, we enter into a new life. Because of God's great mercy, He saves us by washing us clean of our sins...*not because we were good enough to be saved but because of his kindness and pity— by washing away our sins and giving us the new joy of the indwelling Holy Spirit (Titus 3:5 TLB).*

Living victoriously
1 Peter 1:22
Romans 6:6;8:1,4-5,12-14
Galatians 5:25; 6:8
Hebrews 3:13; 12:1
Titus 2:11-12; 3:3-7
2 Corinthians 3:18

Your spirit is washed clean in an instant as the Holy Spirit comes to live within you. This does not mean, however, you will never sin again. Your old nature continues to battle with your new nature, and you have a part to play so you can live victoriously. *So I say, live by the Spirit, and you will not gratify the desires of the sinful nature. For the sinful nature desires what is contrary to the Spirit, and the Spirit what is contrary to the sinful nature. They are in conflict with each other, so that you do not do what you want. But if you are led by the Spirit, you are not under law (Galatians 5:16-18).*

Sinful desires still may tug at you, but now you also have the Holy Spirit pulling you toward holiness. Your very nature has been changed, and it is your new nature to obey God. The power that sin had in your life is now broken and a way of victory is provided: the Holy Spirit helps you to overcome sin. As a Christian, it will be impossible for you to live *habitually* in sin because you are born again into a new life. The Lord will bring to mind any unconfessed sin in your life because He is a merciful God. Suppose I give you a book and three weeks later discover I still have two pages that belong in that book. I make sure you get the pages so you do not miss anything. Similarly, the Lord does not want us to miss anything that would keep us from experiencing a Spirit-led Christian life. He will reveal areas of our lives that need cleansing and help us to become victorious in those areas.

REFLECTION
How do you live victoriously over sin after you become a Christian, according to Galatians 5:16-17?

A man grew up hating a group of neighbors who were of a different nationality. Even after he became a believer, he looked at those people with disdain just because of their nationality. Finally, he read in the scriptures that everyone is on the same footing in the family of God regardless of their background (Romans 10:12). He broke down and repented to God for his sin of hatred toward these people. God gave him a new heart toward his neighbors, and he became friends with several of them. If we are open, God will continue to purify us, change us, and give us victory over sin in our lives.

Trust Jesus to forgive us completely

Remember, when Jesus forgives our sins, He forgives them no matter how many we have committed or how bad they were. All our past sin is gone, wiped spotless by His blood shed on the cross. Blood, in both the Old and New Testaments, stands for death. Christ died, providing a divine substitute for us, as sinners. He became the substitute that would pay the penalty for our sin, permanently! 1 John 1:7 says Jesus' shed blood purifies us from sin. *But if we walk in the light, as he is in the light, we have fellowship with one another, and the blood of Jesus, his Son, purifies us from all sin.*

Forgiveness of sin
Isaiah 43:25
Jeremiah 33:8
Ezekiel 18:22; Acts 3:19
Hebrews 9:28;10:10-18

When our dirty clothes are washed with detergent, they come out spotless. The blood of Jesus is the most potent detergent in the universe. It completely cleanses us from all sin. This purification is an ongoing work of continual cleansing in the life of every believer.

As believers, we will make every effort by His grace to walk in the light so that we can have intimate fellowship with God and each other.

REFLECTION
According to 1 John 1:7, what purifies you from sin? Reflect on how you have experienced God's love and forgiveness of sins.

A woman once washed Jesus' feet with her tears because she was so grateful for the forgiveness of her sins. Jesus said, *...her many sins have been forgiven for she loved much (Luke 7:47).*

Real love for Jesus comes from a deep awareness of our past sinfulness and that He has forgiven us completely. Some say that they have made such terrible mistakes and sinned so horribly that God could never forgive them. No matter what the sin, *everyone* is forgiven for much, because God loves to forgive sin when we repent!

Sins are not remembered

When we repent of our sins, God forgives them and will never remember or mention them again. Psalm 103:12 tells us that *as far as the east is from the west, so far has he removed our transgressions from us.*

You can't get any farther than that! It is as far as you can imagine. When Jesus forgives our sins, He forgets them, period. God gives us a wonderful promise in Micah 7:19. He says He will...*tread our sins underfoot and hurl all our iniquities into the depths of the sea.*

This promise paints an awesome word picture. Our sins sink to the depths of the ocean, never to rise again. God not only casts our sins into the deepest sea, I believe He puts a sign there that says, "No Fishing!"

REFLECTION
When God forgives you of sin, does He ever remember it again? Where does your sin go, according to Micah 7:19?

When the Egyptians pursued the Israelites through the Red Sea, there was not one Egyptian left to pursue God's people. They all perished in the sea Likewise, no sin we have confessed can survive God's forgiveness. Like the Egyptians and their chariots, our sins "...sank like lead in the mighty waters" (Exodus 15:10). Our sins are totally forgiven, never to be remembered again. The Lord has forgotten our sins as if they have never been, and He wants us to forget them too. We are totally set free when Jesus forgives our sins. We can trust Him!

We can count on Him!

Our trust in the Lord is a sure hope or confidence that is based on His promises. We can place our confident hope and trust in the Lord who promises not to disappoint us. *And hope does not disappoint us, because God has poured out his love into our hearts by the Holy Spirit, whom he has given us (Romans 5:5).*

The psalmist puts this "trust" and "hope" into perspective in Psalms 146:3-5 when he says, *Do not put your trust in princes, in mortal men, who cannot save. When their spirit departs, they return to the ground; on that very day their plans come to nothing. Blessed is he whose help is the God of Jacob, whose hope is in the Lord his God.*

We cannot trust mere mortal men, but we can trust our God! We can count on Him to deliver what He has promised. He gives us hope.

REFLECTION

If you trust God, what is His promise (Psalms 146:3-5)? Tell of times you have trusted in the Lord.

I am blessed when my children believe me when I make a promise to them. It would grieve me if they would not trust me. Our heavenly Father feels the same way about us, His children. He has proved Himself faithful to us. We can totally trust Him and His Word. The basis for our trust in God comes from the very nature of God, of Jesus Christ, and His Word. We cannot place our trust in other human beings or material possessions or money or any other thing on this earth. Our abiding trust can only come from the Lord who *does not disappoint us (Romans 5:5).*

CHAPTER 4

Hot, Cold or Lukewarm?

KEY MEMORY VERSE

...I stand at the door and knock.
If anyone hears my voice and opens the door,
I will come in and eat with him,
and he with me.
Revelation 3:20

Neither hot nor cold

Cold:
devoid of
Spiritual
fervor

Hot:
zealous

If we are apathetic about our relationship with Jesus, we are like a glass of lukewarm water, neither hot or cold. Did anyone ever give you a glassful of warm water on a hot summer day when you wanted a refreshing glass of cold water? What a letdown! You probably spit it out of your mouth in disappointment! In the same way, Jesus detests lukewarmness in us.

The Laodicean church was filled with lukewarm Christians who compromised with the world. They professed to be Christians, but they resembled the world more than Christ. Christ said they did not realize it, but they were "wretched, pitiful, poor, blind and naked" (Revelation 3:17).

The Lord warns this church about His judgment against their spiritual condition in Revelation 3:15-17. *I know your deeds, that you are neither cold nor hot. I wish you were either one or the other! So, because you are lukewarm—neither hot nor cold—I am about to spit you out of my mouth.*

Different than a heart willing to change.

God hates lukewarmness. He wants our full commitment rather than a compromise with the world resulting in apathy. Our lukewarmness leaves a bad taste in His mouth, and He will vomit us out! Only place lukewarm is used.

REFLECTION
Why does the Lord detest spiritual lukewarmness? In what ways do you resemble the world more than Christ?

Spiritual compromise

As we just learned, the Lord wants us to completely commit to Him with no compromise. Lukewarmness is repulsive to Him. We cannot try to have one foot in God's kingdom and one foot in the kingdom of darkness. This kind of hypocrisy produces spiritual compromise and displeases God.

Spiritual compromise
2 Corinthians 11:3; 3:14; 10:5

One reason that God is so concerned about lukewarmness is because He knows that people are watching our lives. The Bible says that our lives are like a letter that God writes to people who are watching us. *You yourselves are our letter, written on our hearts, known and read by everybody (2 Corinthians 3:2).*

Our lives are the only Bible that many people ever read. Let's examine our spiritual lives today. Are we lukewarm? If we do not

What does hot look like? Coming to church + learning; turning toward the right people for encouragement; Love

find ourselves hot—excited about the things of God—let's follow the prescription of the Lord. It's found in Revelation 3:19...*become enthusiastic about the things of God (The Living Bible).*

It is our choice. I am choosing to be hot! How about you?

REFLECTION

How is it possible to have one foot in God's kingdom and one in the kingdom of darkness? Why is it important to become enthusiastic about the things of God?

On Purpose!

DAY 3

A way that seems right

There's a story told of a cruise ship with passengers divided into first-class and second-class accommodations. After a few days at sea, the captain announced that from now on, everyone would be treated first-class, no matter what they paid. There would be lobster and fine cuisine for all. The people were excited and gorged themselves on food and exclaimed that he was the greatest captain in the world. Only the captain knew the real truth behind his offer—the ship was sinking and in a short time all would die.

That's the way the devil lies to us. He says, "You can have it all, don't worry—eat, drink and be merry. You can determine your own truth. God doesn't really require that you live a holy life. Everybody else is doing it." But our own wisdom cannot determine wrong and right. Only God's Word can do that. Only by God's Word can we tell if we are on the right path of life. The devil would prefer that we remain blinded and ignorant because he doesn't want people to know that the Bible says, *There is a way that seems right to a man, but in the end it leads to death (Proverbs 14:12).*

In order to determine the right way in life, we must follow God's written revelation in the Bible. Any other path leads us to spiritual death. We cannot allow ourselves to be deceived.

The devil's plan for our lives is to kill us, steal from us, and destroy us. He steals peace, joy, and hope from the lives of those the Lord has created to experi-

REFLECTION

There is a way that may seem right to you, but where is its destination? What can you learn from the cruise ship?

ence true vibrant life. Jesus Christ came to give us life, abundant life, filled with enthusiasm and joy! Jesus said it like this, *The thief does not come except to steal, and to kill, and to destroy. I have come that they may have life, and that they may have it more abundantly (John 10:10 NKJ).*

The Bible tells us that Jesus came to destroy the works of the devil! (1 John 3:8). It seems foolish to not want to be on God's winning team!

Have we turned away from our first love?

When we are spiritually lukewarm, we have turned away from our first love for Jesus. A new love is exciting and vibrant. But love loses its luster when communication wanes. If we no longer communicate in a relationship with our heavenly Father, our love for Him will falter. Perhaps you asked Jesus Christ into your life as your Lord a long time ago, but now you have forsaken your first love for Him.

In Revelation 2:4-5, the Ephesian church had a deep love and devotion to Christ at first, but the Lord warned them that their current relationship with Him was lacking. Although they did a lot of good things and worked hard for the gospel's sake, their heartfelt love for Jesus had died. *...You have forsaken your first love. Remember the height from which you have fallen! Repent and do the things you did at first....*

Just because we knew the Lord in a personal way in the past does not necessarily mean that we have a close relationship with Him today. I was making a point of this truth while speaking at a public high school one time. I asked the students, "Do any of you still know your first grade teacher?" I was startled when a girl in the back of the room raised her hand and said, "Sure I do. She is my mother!" Her point was well taken. The other students, however, had not maintained a relationship with their first grade teacher so their current relationship with her was nonexistent. Do you have a vital relationship with your heavenly Father today? He is still there, waiting for you and me to come back to Him. *Come near to God and he will come near to you... (James 4:8).*

REFLECTION
What does it mean to forsake your first love for Jesus?
If you turn away from your first love, what does the Lord instruct you to do (Revelation 2:5)?

Keep comm. w/ God.
How? Listening more than talking (Classes, Sermons, Seminars, Bible)
blocks? What to do

Biblical Foundations

Backslidden?

He is knocking at your heart's door

Maybe you knew Jesus Christ in a personal way in the past, but you are far from Him today. You have forsaken your once vibrant love for Jesus. In Revelation 3:20, Christ speaks an invitation for the lukewarm people at the church of Laodicea to come back into fellowship with Him. He is pictured as standing outside the door waiting to be invited in once more.

Open the door to Jesus
John 10:7; Matthew 7:7

Jesus is knocking at the door of our lives, waiting for us to repent of our lukewarmness and open the door to invite Him in. Jesus not only warned the Laodicean church of their condition, He immediately invited them to repent and be restored into fellowship with Him again. *...I stand at the door and knock. If anyone hears my voice and opens the door, I will come in and eat with him, and he with me (Revelation 3:20).*

This invitation is spoken outside the door, as Jesus knocks and asks to be readmitted into their presence. He promises that if they repent from their lukewarmness and lack of love for Him, He will completely restore them. What an amazing promise! Jesus wants to have a personal relationship with you today. If you have turned away from God, He wants you to again open the door of your life to Him. And when you open the door, He will come in and again fellowship with you!

REFLECTION
What does the Lord promise if you repent from lukewarmness (Revelation 3:20)?
How has He knocked on your heart's door to bring you back in fellowship with Him?

The power of your testimony

After you receive Jesus Christ as the Lord of your life, it is important to give your testimony as often as possible to as many people as possible. One of the ways you overcome Satan is by speaking out for Christ. Revelation 12:11 says, *they overcame him by the blood of the Lamb and by the word of their testimony....*

There is spiritual power released when we testify how the Lord has changed and is changing our lives! Every Christian has an important personal story to tell of how he or she came to know Jesus Christ as Lord. Never be ashamed to speak for Christ. *So do not be ashamed to testify about our Lord, or ashamed of me his prisoner.*

But join with me in suffering for the gospel, by the power of God, who has saved us and called us to a holy life—not because of anything we have done but because of his own purpose and grace...(2 Timothy 1:8-9).

People will listen when we tell our personal stories of how we came to believe in Jesus. They will not be intimidated because they are not forced to agree or disagree with the statements we make. It is our story, and they cannot deny how we were persuaded to follow Jesus. When we share our stories, we should focus on the fact that God loves them and Jesus died for them so they can be forgiven and be made new. We should tell them of the changes the Lord has made in our lives which gives them hope for their lives, too.

REFLECTION
What should you never be ashamed of? Tell your personal story about how you came to Jesus.
Why is it important to give your testimony as often as possible?

Real or counterfeit?

To some people, Christianity is based on their outward appearance or on what they do rather than a real love for the Lord. They appear righteous outwardly, but inwardly they are not born of God and the Spirit. Jesus sternly reprimanded the Pharisees and scribes in Mark 7:6 for this kind of hypocrisy. *...These people honor me with their lips, but their hearts are far from me.*

For years, I was in the same league as the Pharisees. I considered myself a Christian, but I was living a counterfeit Christian life.

Counterfeit Christianity
Matthew 5:20; 6:1-7
John 3:3-6

Here's my story. My family attended church every Sunday during my childhood. When I was eleven years old, we went to a special evangelistic meeting. I really didn't want to go to hell so I stood up when the evangelist gave an "altar call." I was later water baptized to become part of the church.

What I really wanted that night was "fire insurance." I decided that Christianity would keep me out of hell, but that was as far as it went. My commitment to the Lord was incomplete, so it wasn't long before I was living a fake Christian life. I only acted like a Christian when I was with my Christian friends. (This is also called "hypocrisy.) Seven years later, a friend confronted me: "If you were to die tonight, are you sure you would go to heaven?" I honestly didn't know the answer, so I said, "Nobody knows that."

The young lady didn't hesitate with her answer. She said, "Well, *I* know."

I had come face to face with the truth. Sure, I could talk about God and the Bible. However, I couldn't talk about *Jesus* because I didn't *know* Him in a personal way. I had made a type of commitment to the Lord, but I believed that somehow God would accept me if I did enough good things along the way. I didn't realize that eternal life comes only through faith in Jesus *Christ as Lord.*

Later that night, when I opened my Bible at home, everything seemed to be written directly to me. I read where Jesus said, "You hypocrites!" and I knew I was a hypocrite too. My friends considered me to be "the life of the party," but I knew the truth. Loneliness was my companion every evening that I spent at home alone. Even worse, I was afraid that if I died in the night, I would die without God for eternity. I came to the realization I was under a counterfeit conversion. That night I said, "Jesus, I give You my life. If You can use this rotten, mixed-up life, I'll serve You the rest of my life."

God miraculously changed me the moment I reached out in faith to Him. My attitudes and desires changed. Even my thinking began to change. This time, I was clearly born again because Jesus Christ had become my *Lord.* I was a new creation in Christ, and I am eternally grateful to Jesus.

If you are trying to appear righteous but continue to pursue sinful directions in your heart and mind, you may be living a counterfeit Christian life. Now is the time to ask the Holy Spirit to shine God's light on your heart. Come to the cross of Jesus, confess your sin and accept God's forgiveness.

REFLECTION
How are some professing Christians counterfeit? How can you know the difference?

Pray this prayer of confession and repentance and receive God's unconditional love and forgiveness. *Lord, I have been trapped in the web of hypocrisy and long for the freedom I can have in You. I confess that I have tried to be righteous without You and have been living a counterfeit Christian life. Please forgive my sin so I can come under the power and control and influence of Your righteousness. Thank You for setting me free, Jesus. I pray for courage and wisdom to live out my new life in Christ and experience the fullness and freedom You desire for me to have.*

Building a Solid Foundation

1. Foundation of Jesus Christ

1 Corinthians 3:11

> *Ex: The first step in building a house—putting in a solid foundation.*

a. Jesus claims to be the way, the truth, the life (John 14:6).

b. How is it possible to know all about God but not really know Him personally?

> *Ex: You may know about the Queen of England but probably do not know her personally.*

c. God is revealed to us personally through Jesus Christ John 17:3

2. God wants to know us personally!

a. God intended for the beauty of the universe to point to Him. Psalms 19:1; Romans 1:20

b. Can God's existence be proved? No, accepted by faith. Hebrews 11:6

c. Why does God seek mankind? To reflect His image and fellowship with us (Genesis 1:26).

3. Jesus—The only way to God

a. Why were you created? God created man without sin and to have a perfect relationship with Him.

b. After Adam and Eve rebelled, sin alienated man from God. Genesis 3:6, 14-19

c. How can we know God? Through Jesus Christ. John 14:7,9

4. Realize we are lost in our sins

Romans 3:23

a. Sin is missing the mark of God's perfect will.

Ex: Impossible to always hit the bull's eye

D. L. Moody story of one weak link.

b. Jesus came to solve the sin problem of mankind, first convicting us of sin (John 16:8), then, we must believe Jesus can save us from our sin (John 3:18).

5. Repent and believe

a. God does not want to see us perish in sin (2 Peter 3:9).

b. What wages do sins pay? The death penalty (Romans 6:23), but God offers the free gift of salvation and eternal life.

c. Repent and believe in the good news (Mark 1:14-15).

d. *Repentance* means *to change, turn around, transform.*

e. Repentance is turning from everything we know is displeasing to God—an unconditional surrender.

6. Confess Jesus as Lord

Romans 10:9

Ex: Just as a couple confesses their commitment to each other on their wedding day, to begin our relationship with   God, we confess Jesus Christ as Lord.

a. *Lord* means *ruler, king, boss.* What does having Jesus as Lord mean to you?

b. Someday everyone will kneel before the Lord.

Philippians 2:10-11

7. Receive salvation and become God's child!

a. Jesus took our place on the cross so we can know God.

1 Peter 3:18

b. You must receive Him to become His child (John 1:12). What is the difference between believing and receiving Christ?

Ex: Money offered to teenager. He can believe it is his, but he must also receive it.

c. Have you asked Jesus Christ into your life? Now is the day of salvation (2 Corinthians 6:2).

Counting the Cost

1. Total commitment required

a. "Call on the Lord, be saved" (Romans 10:13). Calling on the Lord requires total commitment.

b. Sometimes Christians preach a "weak" Jesus. Count the cost (Luke 14:33).

   Ex: Youth leader changes his approach to "Jesus must be Lord over all" and sees lasting fruit.

c. In what ways did you count the cost before you made a commitment to Christ?

2. Consider the cost

a. Seriously consider what it involves to follow Him.
Luke 14:28-29

b. Luke 14:26 What does it mean to hate family members, including our own lives? Devotion to family must take second place to devotion to Christ.

   Ex: Jewish woman was rejected by family when she was saved. Understood giving up all to follow Christ.

   Ex: Charles Finney told students to count the cost first. Their commitment lasted.

3. Bear the cross
Luke 14:27,33

   Ex: Story of the chicken and pig.

a. Bearing the cross of Christ is symbolic of dying to self.

b. When you die to your sins, you save your life!
Luke 9:23-24

c. How has losing your life for Jesus actually saved it?

4. Jesus must be Lord of everything

a. Matthew 19:16-22 Rich young ruler lacked total commitment to the Lord. **Either Jesus is Lord of all or not Lord at all!**

Ex: Can't keep glove compartment! How do we try to keep "glove compartments" for ourselves?

b. Why are some people frustrated and unfulfilled? Our lives can only be filled with purpose when Jesus gives us real life! 1 John 5:11-12

5. Sell out!

a. Jesus expects us to sell out completely to His lordship. Parable of the Pearl (Matthew 13:45-46). How much was the pearl worth?

b. We were bought with a price (1 Corinthians 6:20) and should be willing to sacrifice all things for Christ.

Ex: Disciples gave up their boats, nets, tax collector position (their livelihood) to follow Jesus.

c. How do we give everything to the Lord?

6. It all belongs to Him

a. Earthly things can enslave us (Luke 12:34). What are some things people are enslaved to today?

b. Jesus is the owner, we are the managers. How do you manage, rather than own, earthly things?

Ex: Story of Argentine Christians who sold homes to give to the church...but got them back to manage.

7. How to be spiritually reborn

a. Nicodemus learned what rebirth was—being changed from the inside out (John 3:3). Why is is so important to be spiritually reborn?

b. Start living the new life of Christ who lives in you! Galatians 2:20

c. How has the Lord changed your heart?

Total Trust

1. The difference between belief and trust

    a. Believe in Jesus to have eternal life (John 3:16).

    b. Many people believe but do not fully trust. Even the devil believes in Jesus! (James 2:19).

        Ex: Children trust to jump into father's arms.

        Ex: Tightrope walker over Niagara falls.

    c. Being sincere is not enough. You may be sincerely wrong.

        Ex: Man traveling (sincerely) in wrong direction.

2. We trust God because He is God!

    a. Trust Him because we love Him.

    b. Paul reveals his trust in Christ (2 Timothy 1:12).

    c. Don't trust God for His benefits, although He will "load us with benefits" (Psalms 68:19).

        Ex: Wrong reasons to serve God: Man serves God, hoping to marry a certain girl.

    d. Anything that means more to us than Jesus is an idol.
1 John 5:21

        What are some idols we may have in our lives?

    e. As we trust the Lord, He will fill us with joy and peace.
Romans 15:13

3. We cannot trust our feelings

        Ex: Sometimes we feel close to God and others times feel far away. Why are feelings so unreliable?

    a. God wants us to know we have eternal life (1 John 5:13).

    b. Think of ourselves according to what God says about us, not by how we feel. We are being changed and renewed.
Ephesians 4:22-24

4. What If I don't change completely after I give my life to Jesus?

a. When you become a Christian, your spirit is washed clean. Titus 3:5

b. How to live victoriously over sin? Sinful desires may tug, but Holy Spirit empowers us to overcome (Galatians 5:16-18).

Ex: Book with missing pages story.

Ex: A racist man becomes a Christian and discovers God can change his heart.

5. Trust Jesus to forgive us completely

a. What purifies us from sin? Jesus' blood (1 John 1:7).

b. Love for Jesus comes from a deep awareness of past sinfulness and knowing we are forgiven completely. Luke 7:47

c. Reflect on how you have experienced God's love and forgiveness of sin.

6. Sins are not remembered

a. When God forgives sins, not remembered (Psalms 103:12).

b. Where does our sin go? In the deepest ocean (Micah 7:19).

Ex: The Egyptians perished in the sea (Exodus 15:10) like our sins.

7. We can count on Him!

a. Our trust in the Lord is a sure hope.

b. God will never disappoint (Romans 5:5).

c. Never trust mortal men, only God (Psalms 146:3-5).

d. God will deliver what He promised.

Ex: I am blessed when my children believe me when I make a promise to them. God feels the same way.

Hot, Cold or Lukewarm?

1. **Neither hot nor cold**
   a. Jesus detests lukewarmness (Revelation 3:15-17).
   b. Laodicean church filled with lukewarm Christians who compromised with world. How do some Christians resemble the world more than Christ?

2. **Spiritual compromise**
   a. One foot in God's kingdom and in the kingdom of darkness produces spiritual compromise. Name possible ways to have one foot in two kingdoms.
   b. Why is it important to become enthusiastic about God? Our lives are the "Bible" people read (2 Corinthians 3:2).
   c. Not enthusiastic about the things of God (Revelation 3:19)? People will not want what we have.

3. **A way that seems right**
   Ex: Cruise ship story. What can we learn?
   a. A way may seem right to us, but where is its destination? Devil wants us to remain ignorant of Bible truths (Proverbs 14:12).
   b. Follow God's written revelation in the Bible.
   c. Jesus came to give abundant life (John 10:10) and destroy works of devil (1 John 3:8).

4. **Have we turned away from our first love?**
   a. The Ephesian church turned away from their first love for Jesus (Revelation 2:4-5). What does it mean to forsake your first love?
   b. What does the Lord instruct us to do? Repent.
   c. Do you have a vital relationship with Jesus? (James 4:8).

5. He is knocking at your heart's door

a. God invites lukewarm Christians back into fellowship (Revelation 3:20). What does the Lord promise if we repent from lukewarmness?

b. If you have backslidden, the Lord wants you to again open the door of your life to Him. Has He knocked on your heart's door?

6. The power of your testimony

a. Why is it important to give our testimony as often as possible? Defeat the powers of darkness by testifying how Christ has changed us (Revelation 12:11).

b. What should we never be ashamed of?
To speak for Christ (2 Timothy 1:8-9).

c. Every Christian has a personal story to tell of how he came to Christ.

As a teacher, this would be a good time to give your personal testimony to the group.

7. Real or counterfeit?

a. To some, Christianity is based on outward appearances rather than a real love for the Lord.
See Matthew 5:20; 6:1-7; John 3:3-6.

b. These people honor God with their lips, but their hearts are far from Him (Mark 7:6).
Ex: Story of counterfeit conversion.

c. How are some professing Christians counterfeit?
How can we know the difference?

Chapter 1
Building a Solid Foundation
Journaling space for reflection questions

DAY 1 *How is it possible to know all about God but not really know Him? According to John 14:6, how can you know God?*

DAY 2 *You can see God in nature, but how can you truly believe that He exists (Hebrews 11:6)? Why does God seek mankind?*

DAY 3 *Why were you created? What alienates you from God? How can you know God, according to John 14:9?*

DAY 4

What evidence have you seen in your experience or observation that convinces you humanity is lost?

DAY 5

What wages does sin pay according to Romans 6:23? Describe "repentance" in your own words.

DAY 6

What does having Jesus as the Lord of your life mean to you personally?

DAY 7

What is the difference between believing and receiving Christ? Salvation is a free gift—Do you want to receive God's gift of Jesus Christ?

Chapter 2
Counting the Cost
Journaling space for reflection questions

In what ways did you count the cost before you made a commitment to Christ?

What does it mean to "hate" family members, including your own life before you can become a disciple of Jesus (Luke 14:26)?

In your experience, how has losing your life for Jesus actually saved it?

How do you try to keep "glove compartments" for yourself?

In the Parable of the Pearl, how much was the pearl worth? How do you give everything to the Lord?

What are some things that enslave people today?
How do you manage, rather than own, earthly things?

Why is it so important to be spiritually reborn?
How has the Lord changed your heart?

Chapter 3
Total Trust
Journaling space for reflection questions

In your own words, explain the difference between mentally believing in Jesus vs. trusting fully in Him.

What are some idols you may have in your life?
Why do you serve God?

Why are feelings so unreliable?
How has God's Word caused faith to rise up in your life?

How do you live victoriously over sin after you become a Christian, according to Galatians 5:16-17?

According to 1 John 1:7, what purifies you from sin? Reflect on how you have experienced God's love and forgiveness of sins.

When God forgives you of sin, does He ever remember it again? Where does your sin go, according to Micah 7:19?

If you trust God, what is His promise (*Psalms 146:3-5*)?
Tell of times you have trusted in the Lord.

Chapter 4
Hot, Cold or Lukewarm?
Journaling space for reflection questions

DAY 1

Why does the Lord detest spiritual lukewarmness?
In what ways do you resemble the world more than Christ?

DAY 2

How is it possible to have one foot in God's kingdom and one in the kingdom of darkness? Why is it important for you to become enthusiastic about the things of God?

DAY 3

There is a way that may seem right to you, but where is its destination? What can you learn from the cruise ship?

DAY 4

What does it mean to forsake our first love for Jesus?
If you turn away from your first love, what does the Lord instruct you to do (Revelation 2:5)?

DAY 5

What does the Lord promise if you repent from lukewarmness (Revelation 3:20)? How has He knocked on your heart's door to bring you back in fellowship with Him?

DAY 6

What should you never be ashamed of?
Tell your personal story about how you came to Jesus.
Why is it important to give your testimony as often as possible?

DAY 7

How are some professing Christians counterfeit?
How can you know the difference?

Daily Devotional Extra Days

If you are using this book as a daily devotional, you will notice there are 28 days in this study. Depending on the month, you may need the three extra days' studies given here.

DAY 29

Whose Treasure?

Read Luke 12:16-21. What did the rich man say to himself? What did God say? How can you fall into this same trap?

DAY 30

Which Gate?

Read Matthew 7:13-14. What is the difference between the narrow gate and the wide gate? Explain this illustration about the two gates from your own personal experience.
Who makes the choice as to which gate you enter?

DAY 31

Not Ashamed?

Read Mark 8:36-38. How do you answer the questions that Jesus asked in these verses? If you are ashamed of Jesus, what does He tell us about your future (unless you confess your sin to Him and receive His cleansing)?
What do these verses teach you about your priorities?

Coordinates with this series!

Biblical Foundations for Children

Creative learning experiences for ages 4-12, patterned after the *Biblical Foundation Series*, with truths in each lesson. Takes kids on the first steps in their Christian walk by teaching them how to build solid foundations in their young lives. *by Jane Nicholas, 176 pages:* $17.95

Other books by Larry Kreider

Hearing God 30 Different ways

The Lord speaks to us in ways we often miss. He has many ways of speaking, including through the Bible, prayer, circumstances, spiritual gifts, conviction, His character, His peace, and even in times of silence.

30 ways in 30 days Take the next 30 days, reading a chapter each day, to explore ways God speaks. Expect to be surprised! Use as a personal devotional or go through this material with your small group or congregation. *by Larry Kreider, 224 pages:* $14.99

The Cry for Spiritual Fathers & Mothers

Returning to the biblical truth of spiritual parenting so believers are not left fatherless and disconnected. How loving, seasoned spiritual fathers and mothers help spiritual children reach their full potential in Christ. *by Larry Kreider, 186 pages*: $11.95

The Biblical Role of Elders for Today's Church

New Testament leadership principles for equipping elders. What elders' qualifications and responsibilities are, how they are chosen, how elders are called to be armor bearers, spiritual fathers and mothers, resolving conflicts, and more. *by Larry Kreider, Ron Myer, Steve Prokopchak, and Brian Sauder.* $12.99

Visit www.h2hp.com for more information

Hearing God 30 Different Ways

Learn to "tune in" to God and discern "HIS" voice. God wants to speak to you. Includes a seminar manual.

Spiritual Fathering & Mothering Seminar

Practical preparation for believers who want to have and become spiritual parents. Includes a seminar manual.

Elder's Training Seminar

Based on New Testament leadership principles, this seminar equips leaders to provide protection, direction and correction in the local church. Includes a seminar manual.

Small Groups 101 Seminar

Basics for healthy cell ministry. Session topics cover the essentials for growing cell group ministry. Each attendee receives a *Helping You Build Manual*.

Small Groups 201 Seminar

Takes you beyond the basics and into an advanced strategy for cell ministry. Each attendee receives a seminar manual.

Counseling Basics

This seminar takes you through the basics of counseling, specifically in small group ministry and others. Includes a comprehensive manual.

Marriage Mentoring Training Seminar

Trains church leaders and mature believers to help prepare engaged couples for a strong marriage foundation by using the mentoring format of *Called Together*. Includes a *Called Together Manual*.

Seminars held at various locations throughout the US and Canada. For complete brochures and upcoming dates:

Call 1.800.848.5892
www.dcfi.org   email: info@dcfi.org